Technology through the Ages

COMPUTING
THROUGH THE AGES
From Bones to Binary

MICHAEL WOODS AND MARY B. WOODS

T0054214

TWENTY-FIRST CENTURY BOOKS™ / MINNEAPOLIS

For Clara Starr

Twenty-First Century Books™
An imprint of Lerner Publishing Group, Inc.
241 First Avenue North
Minneapolis, MN 55401 USA

For reading levels and more information, look up this title at www.lernerbooks.com.

Main body text set in Bembo Std Regular
Typeface provided by Monotype Typography.

Library of Congress Cataloging-in-Publication Data

The Cataloging-in-Publication Data for *Computing through the Ages: From Bones to Binary* is on file at the Library of Congress.
ISBN 979-8-7656-1004-6 (lib. bdg.)
ISBN 979-8-7656-2521-7 (pbk.)
ISBN 979-8-7656-1941-4 (epub)

Manufactured in the United States of America
1 – CG – 12/15/23

CONTENTS

INTRODUCTION

What do you think of when you hear the word *technology*? You probably think of computers, smartphones, and the latest scientific tools. But technology doesn't just mean brand-new machines and discoveries. Technology is as old as human civilization.

Technology is the use of knowledge, inventions, and discoveries to make life better. The word *technology* comes from Greek. *Téchnē* means "art" or "craft." The suffix -*logia* means the study of arts and crafts. In modern times, technology refers to a craft, a technique, or a tool.

People use technology to farm crops, construct buildings, and get from place to place. This book looks at a technology that has been used to accomplish these tasks: computing.

What Is Computing?

Computing is the process of using numbers to count, gather information, and solve problems. It involves manipulating numbers by adding, subtracting, multiplying, and dividing

Over time, computer scientists were able to fit advanced computing technology into devices that fit in a person's hand.

them. For most of history, humans used their own brains to compute and solve problems with the aid of measuring and counting tools. Even by the twentieth century, the word *computer* was usually used to describe a person who computes, not a machine. It was only very recently that humans began using machines to compute.

Computing involves mathematics—the science of numbers and how they relate to one another. Math has many branches and many practical applications. It is used in every industry and area of science, from graphic design to manufacturing to medicine.

This cave painting from prehistoric Mexico was painted in around 7500 BCE. The human figures are shown with hands and fingers raised. Early peoples probably used fingers and toes to keep track of quantities.

Ancient Roots

Computing probably began shortly after the first humans appeared on Earth. The first computing technologies were simple, but they were accurate and easy to learn. Early peoples performed mathematics by counting on their fingers and toes. They kept track of numbers by cutting notches into sticks and tying knots in ropes.

Ancient peoples discovered some computing methods by trial and error. Sometimes people copied and improved on computing technology used in other parts of the world. The ancient Greeks, for instance, learned about geometry from the Egyptians and the Babylonians. The Romans learned from the Greeks. Each civilization found new ways to do more complex computing. Gradually, computing knowledge spread throughout the world. Mathematics became a universal language.

Archaeologists learn about ancient computing knowledge through the writings and carvings people left behind. Ancient tools and monuments can give clues about computing knowledge too. Greek water clocks show how precisely the Greeks could tell time. In Central America, dates inscribed on stone monuments give insight into the calendar systems of the ancient Maya culture. Clues like these tell scientists how ancient peoples counted, measured, and calculated.

A Lot with a Little

Ancient computing methods have stood the test of time. We measure angles in degrees, minutes, and seconds thanks to the ancient Babylonians. We divide our day into twenty-four hours, just as the ancient Egyptians did. Our number symbols were created in ancient India. We sometimes use Roman numerals, which were developed in Rome more than two thousand years ago.

Ancient people used math for fun too. They developed number games, tricks, and puzzles. Read on and discover some of the incredible computing knowledge we have inherited from people who lived long ago.

CHAPTER ONE

Computing Basics

The first modern humans on Earth lived about 300,000 years ago. They lived in small groups and got their food by hunting game, fishing, and gathering wild plants. When the food in one area was all used up, the group moved to a new place. They made tools from stone, wood, animal bones, plant fibers, and clay.

Early hunter-gatherers probably knew the importance of quantities, or amounts. They knew that two antelopes meant more food than one. A pack of wolves was more dangerous than a lone wolf. A bunch of berries was more valuable than one berry. But did early hunter-gatherers understand the ideas behind numbers?

Finger Symbols

We can only guess about when humans developed basic systems for counting. They probably used fingers to represent numbers. One finger was probably the universal symbol for one, two fingers for two, and so on. It's no surprise that our modern

The Ishango bone is a tally stick that dates to around 25,000 BCE. This bone, which may have come from a primate's upper thigh, is carved with notches. Archaeologists found the bone in 1950 in central Africa.

numbering system is based on ten—the number of human fingers. In fact, the word *digit*, meaning a single numeral, also refers to a finger or a toe.

Sticks and Bones

Archaeologists have found ancient tally sticks made of wood and bones, with rows of neatly cut notches from as early as 35000 BCE. Ancient peoples kept track of numbers with these notches. A tally stick known as the Lebombo bone was carved around this time. The stick was a baboon bone discovered near a cave in Swaziland, in southern Africa, in the 1970s. Someone carved twenty-nine notches into the bone.

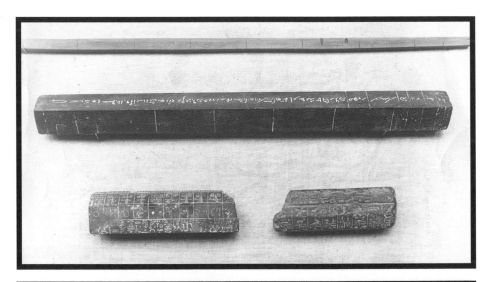

These examples of Egyptian cubit rods of basalt (volcanic rock) and wood date from between 1600 and 250 BCE. The Egyptian cubit was divided into seven "palms" of four "digits," making twenty-eight parts in all. A cubit measured around 20.6 inches (52.3 cm) in length.

Also known as mancala or oware, ayo (pronounced AH-yoh) originated in western Nigeria thousands of years ago. Players use seeds, beans, or marbles to play the counting game, which requires quick thinking and math skills.

Measuring with Body Parts

Ancient peoples also measured with other parts of the human body. They used their feet to measure distances. For thousands of years, the unit called the foot was not a fixed length. It varied depending on the size of the person's foot doing the measurement.

Other ancient units of measurement used this same idea. One of the most widely used was the cubit. The cubit was the distance from a person's elbow to the tip of their middle finger. The width of a person's thumb became the first measure of an inch. Later, one inch meant the length of an index finger from the tip to the first joint. A hand was the width of a person's hand. People still use hands to measure the height of horses.

CHAPTER TWO
The Ancient Middle East

Around 3500 BCE, some people in the Middle East began building houses, farms, and villages. They farmed fertile land between the Tigris and Euphrates rivers. This region was known as Mesopotamia. Mesopotamia was home to many ancient cultures over several thousand years. These included the Sumerians, Babylonians, Hittites, and Assyrians.

As people in the Middle East settled into farming villages, they needed ways to mark the boundaries of their land. They developed a technology called surveying. Surveying uses math to measure distances, angles, and geologic features such as hills and rivers. With surveying techniques, people could determine the areas and borders of a farmer's land. Ancient mapmakers could accurately show rivers, hills, and other land features. Surveying was also important in construction. It helped ancient engineers design straight roads, buildings, and bridges.

Writings and other artifacts from the Sumerians show that people in the ancient Middle East measured land boundaries as early as 1400 BCE. The Sumerians also used this technology to pick the location of streets and buildings in their cities.

This relief carving from the Assyrian Palace at Nineveh (in modern-day Iraq), ca. 650 BCE, shows farmers harvesting sugarcane on the banks of a river. People of the ancient Middle East used numbers and computing techniques to calculate sizes of plots of land.

The First Salespeople

Farmers in the ancient Middle East were perhaps the world's first salespeople. Mesopotamia had excellent farmland. Farmers produced more food than they needed, so they were able to sell the surplus.

Babylon was a commercial center. At markets, merchants traded grain, dried fish, cloth, brick, and gold with people from many other cities. To set prices, merchants

13

needed standard units of money, length, and weight.
The Mesopotamians used the cubit for many of their
measurements. They divided the cubit into two feet, and each
foot into three hands.

Computing Weight

Archaeologists think the first scale was invented in either ancient
Babylonia or ancient Egypt. Both civilizations used scales,
perhaps as early as 5000 BCE.

Ancient scales were beam scales. They were made from
a stick or a rod balanced upon a center support. A pan hung

Beam scales start out in a neutral position, as shown here. When objects
are placed on the plates, the scale's balance tips until the weights on both
sides match.

Sets of standard weights like these were used with beam scales in Ur (modern-day southern Iraq) ca. 1900–1600 BCE. The weights are made from a stone called hematite.

from each end of the beam. When an object in one pan was heavier than an object in the other, one pan hung lower on that side. When the objects were equal in weight, the pans balanced.

The first beam scales simply compared the weight of two different objects. They didn't measure an object's weight based on standard units. The Babylonians eventually developed the world's first weight standards —units of measurement that were the same from place to place.

The Babylonian standards were smooth stones. They were ground and polished to make sure each weighed the same. The stones had a standard weight. Merchants placed one or more stones on one pan of a beam scale. They placed objects to be bought or sold in the other. They might have weighed out two stones' worth of grain, for example. With standardized weights, business transactions were more consistent. Similar beam scales are still used for measurements that do not require precise accuracy.

Computing Time

Sundials are devices that measure time by the position of the sun as it moves across the sky. Sundials can be very accurate timekeepers. Of course, they aren't useful at night or on cloudy days. But sundials helped ancient peoples to measure time in daylight.

The ancient Babylonians made some of the world's first sundials. They were flat pieces of stone or wood with an upright bar in the center called a gnomon. The gnomon cast a shadow on the dial. As the earth rotates, the sun's position changes in the sky. As the sun's position changed, the shadow cast by the gnomon moved across the lines on the dial. Each line stood for a certain time of day.

Around 300 BCE, a Babylonian astronomer named Berosus made a sundial with a curved base. It was shaped like a bowl. The gnomon stood in the center of the bowl. Lines on the bottom of the bowl divided each day into twelve equal parts. These were the first hours. Clocks like this were used for more than a thousand years. Berosus started our modern system of twenty-four-hour days, with days and nights each twelve hours long.

Counting by 60s

People in the ancient Middle East were some of the first known people to create symbols for numbers. A different symbol stood for a collection of two, three, four, and so on. Archaeologists

Sundials similar to the one pictured here were used for many centuries to keep track of hours, days, and seasons.

have found clay tablets thousands of years old marked with numbers in the ruins of ancient Middle Eastern cities.

The Mesopotamian numeral system was based on the number sixty. We still use this system to measure time. Symbols on the tablets stood for 1 through 59. The symbol for 1 also stood for 60 or 3600, depending on its place in a number. Sound confusing? It's not really. In the same way, we can use a 1 to stand for 100, as in the number 156. This kind of numeral system is called a place-value system.

A Famous Number

One of the most useful numbers to engineers, physicists, and other scientists is pi, represented by the symbol π. Multiplying pi by the diameter of a circle—the distance across its middle—gives you the circle's circumference, which is the distance around the outside.

The ancient Babylonians and Egyptians discovered pi around 2000 BCE. They found it by studying how the circumference of a circle changes as its diameter changes. Babylonian mathematicians figured that pi was equal to 3.125. Egyptians figured the number at 3.160. Modern mathematicians define pi as approximately 3.14159.

Pi (π): What We've Learned Since Ancient Times

As far as mathematicians know, pi is an infinite decimal. This means that, after the decimal point, the digits go on forever. Modern computers have figured pi's value to nearly three trillion decimal places. But the fewer decimals that ancient mathematicians used were close enough for their purposes.

This tablet, dated around 500 BCE, records astronomical information observed by the ancient Babylonians, such as stars and constellations.

CHAPTER THREE
Ancient Egypt

People in ancient Egypt began to settle along the Nile River around 7000 BCE. The ancient Egyptians built giant pyramids, devised a picture-writing system called hieroglyphics, and developed medical techniques that were studied and shared around the ancient world.

The ancient Egyptians used computing technology for many projects. They used addition and subtraction to keep track of taxes, accounts, and trade transactions. They used math to survey and measure fields. They measured time with sundials and other clocks. They used engineering techniques, such as measuring and calculating right angles, to build the Great Pyramid of Giza so each side aligned with one of the four cardinal directions.

Ancient Textbooks

In the 1800s, archaeologists discovered two textbooks that were used in schools in ancient Egypt to teach scribes. Scribes were professionals trained to read, write, and perform equations. Both

The ancient Egyptians settled along the Nile River (*above*). They developed hieroglyphic writing and numbers to record history, keep track of business, and execute construction projects, among other things.

textbooks were long scrolls of paper made from papyrus.

The Rhind Mathematical Papyrus is our most important source of information about Egyptian math. It was named for Alexander Henry Rhind, a Scottish archaeologist. He purchased the scroll near the Egyptian city of Thebes in 1858.

An Egyptian scribe, Ahmes the Moonborn, wrote the papyrus around 1650 BCE. He called it "insight into all that exists, knowledge of all secrets." The papyrus explained how to add, subtract, and do other computations with whole numbers and fractions. Ahmes also included more advanced math in his textbook. One was algebra. This branch of

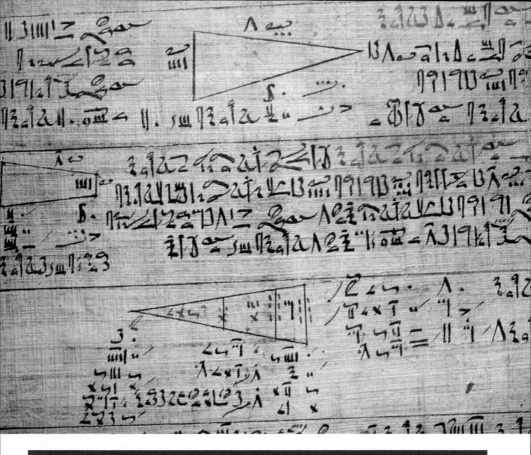

The Rhind Mathematical Papyrus dates to the 1600s BCE. Experts began to translate the mathematical text in the late 1800s.

math uses symbols to stand for numbers. One simple algebra equation is 6 + x = 7. To solve the equation, you must find the value of x. In this case, the answer is x = 1.

The Egyptians used algebra to solve practical problems. For instance, suppose one thousand stonecutters were building a pyramid. Each stonecutter eats three loaves of bread a day. How much bread would be needed to feed the stonecutters for ten days? The equation might look like this: x = 1,000 x 3 x 10. That's 30,000 loaves!

The Moscow Mathematical Papyrus, another ancient Egyptian scroll, was used in the 1800s BCE. It is named for

Russia's capital city, where it is kept. The scroll is sometimes called the Golenishchev Papyrus, after the man who bought it in Egypt in the 1890s CE. The author is unknown. Like the Rhind Papyrus, the Moscow Papyrus included practical arithmetic and algebra problems. The Moscow Papyrus also included geometry. In one problem, students had to find the volume of a pyramid with its top missing.

Strange Multiplying and Dividing

Ancient Egyptian computing methods changed over several thousand years. One way the Egyptians multiplied numbers may seem quite strange to modern students. In the Old Kingdom period (about 2650 to 2150 BCE), Egyptians used two columns of numbers. The left column always began with 1 and doubled with each row. The right column began with the number to be multiplied and doubled with each row. Suppose a student wanted to multiply thirty by twelve. The student first made two columns:

1	30
2	60
4	120
8	240
16	480

The student would then write down numbers from the first column that added up to twelve: 4 + 8 = 12. Then the student would add the "partners" of those numbers from the next column to get the answer: 120 + 240 = 360.

Egyptian scribes recorded information on crop yields, tax collection, building projects, and much more. This detail is from a wall painting in the tomb of Mennah, an important scribe from about 1400 BCE.

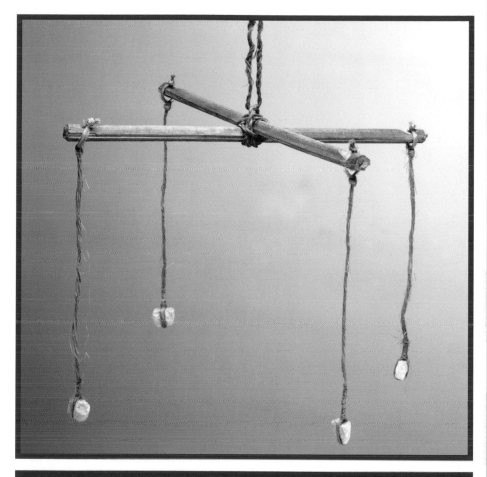

This groma, used for measuring right angles, dates to the first century BCE. It was found during an excavation of the ancient Egyptian Fayum Province in 1899.

Great Surveyors

It took careful surveying to build the Great Pyramid of Giza, completed around 2560 BCE. The pyramid was 481 feet (147 m) high and was built from more than two million stone blocks. Its base is 755 feet (230 m) long on each side and covers an area

> "For the Egyptians
> had to perform
> [land] measurements
> because the overflow
> of the Nile would
> cause the boundary
> of each person's land
> to disappear. . . . The
> discovery both of
> [geometry] and of the
> other sciences proceeded
> from utility."
>
> —Proclus Lycius, Greek
> philosopher, 410–485 CE

nearly the size of ten football fields. Yet the sides of the base come within 7 inches (18 cm) of forming a perfect square. The sides are almost exactly aligned to face the cardinal directions—north, south, east, and west.

How did Egyptian surveyors work so accurately? Part of their secret was a tool called the groma. They used it to make right angles. The groma was a flat wooden cross. Its arms intersected in the middle to form four right angles. Cords were attached at both ends of each arm. Weights were tied to the cords. When the cross was horizontal, the weighted cords hung straight down, forming right angles with the arms of the cross. Ancient surveyors lined up the groma's arms and cords with the walls and ceilings of buildings. Gromas helped builders make sure that the walls formed perfect right angles with one another.

The Nilometer

The Nile's yearly flooding was important to Egyptian farmers. Too little flooding meant less water for crops and a bad harvest. Too much flooding could damage farms and cities. Around 3000 BCE, the Egyptians created a device for computing the Nile's flood. Archaeologists call it the Nilometer.

Visitors to Cairo, Egypt, can tour the Nilometer on Roda Island. As the Nile's water level rises, marks on the wooden post measure its height. Most of the structure that was built in 715 CE was destroyed by floodwaters. The existing nilometer was rebuilt in 1092.

Nilometers were stone pillars or steps along the riverbanks marked with measurements. They measured the water level when the Nile overflowed.

Measuring with Grain

One of the smallest units of weight in the United States and the United Kingdom is the grain. A grain is tiny. It takes 437.5 grains to equal 1 ounce (28 g) and 7,000 grains to equal 1 pound (0.45 kg).

The ancient Egyptians first used this unit of measurement thousands of years ago. It originally equaled the weight of one grain of wheat. Merchants selling small amounts of precious goods, such as gold, would put several grains of wheat on one side of a beam scale. They weighed out enough goods on the other side to make both sides balance.

This scene from a wall in the tomb of Mereruka, a powerful Egyptian official, shows merchants measuring goods with a beam scale.

Shadow Clocks, Sundials, and Water Clocks

Like the Babylonians, the Egyptians divided daylight into twelve equal parts. The Egyptians used clocks as early as 3500 BCE. The first Egyptian clock was an obelisk, a tall, four-sided pillar. It cast a shadow as the sun moved past. The shadow grew shorter throughout the morning and disappeared at noon with the sun directly overhead. The shadow lengthened throughout the afternoon. People estimated the time based on the length of the shadow.

Sometime around 1500 BCE, the Egyptians made a more precise sundial called a shadow clock. It looked like the letter T stuck in the ground. A long, narrow base extended behind it along the ground. Lines on the base marked the hours. Egyptians could tell the time of day by looking at which line the bar's shadow reached. Later, they used sundials in the shape of half circles, like those in the ancient Middle East. But in Egypt, as in most places, the amount of daylight changes with the seasons. Each hour was longer in the summer and shorter in the winter.

Egyptians also invented the clepsydra, or water clock, around 1500 BCE. It was a clay jar with markings on the inside with a small hole at the bottom. Unlike sundials, water clocks could keep time at night. As water in the jar dribbled out, more and more markings became visible. Each mark showed that another unit of time had passed. Clepsydras had to be made very precisely so they all kept time the same. Water had to flow out of each one at about the same rate.

This replica of an ancient Egyptian water clock is based on the original version carved from alabaster stone. There are ten columns of twelve indentations around the inside of the clock.

Summer in December?

The solar year is the time the earth takes to travel around the sun. It takes approximately 365 days, five hours, forty-eight minutes, and forty-six seconds. What would happen if a calendar didn't match the solar year? Holidays and seasons would gradually shift. June, July, and August would eventually fall in the middle of winter instead of summer.

At first, ancient calendars did shift in this way. That's because they were created to align with the lunar year, which is divided into twelve months based on the phases of the moon. It lasts only 354 days. These first calendars did not stay aligned with the seasons over long periods. They shifted 110 days—almost four months—every ten years.

The Egyptians were the first people to create a calendar based on the solar year. Their calendar had twelve months of thirty days each, with five extra days added at the end of each year. In 238 BCE, the pharaoh Ptolemy III made the calendar even more consistent. He added an extra day every fourth year. That day made up for the nearly six-hour difference between the calendar year and the solar year. A year with an extra day is now called a leap year.

Picture Numbers

Ancient Egyptians wrote words with hieroglyphics, which uses pictures instead of letters. They also used it to write numbers. In the Egyptian system, a single line stood for one, two lines for two, three lines for three, and so on up to nine. An archlike symbol stood for ten. A spiral represented one hundred. The number one thousand was represented by a lotus plant. A picture of an index finger meant ten thousand. The picture for one hundred thousand was a tadpole or a frog. A person sitting with arms upraised stood for one million. To write the number 1,109, an Egyptian scribe would draw a lotus plant (1,000), a spiral (100), and nine lines (9).

CHAPTER FOUR
Ancient India

People in modern-day Pakistan, Afghanistan, and northwestern India began settling into villages along the Indus River valley around 4000 BCE. During the next thousand years, they developed a thriving society known today as the Indus Valley Civilization.

Evidence shows that the Indus Valley Civilization lasted from 2500 to 1500 BCE. We still do not know why the civilization collapsed. But we do know that the ancient Indians introduced several advances in computing technology. Later groups of people in India also made important developments in computing.

Arabic Numerals = Indian Numerals

The numbers we use today originated in ancient India. These Hindu-Arabic numerals came from ancient Indian symbols. The oldest known Indian numbering system used Brahmi numerals. This system allowed people to write down any number, no matter how big, with just ten symbols. These

Mohenjo-daro, built around 2600 BCE, was one of the largest settlements of the Indus Valley Civilization. The ruins, discovered in 1922, are located in modern-day Pakistan.

symbols represented the numbers one through nine. The first known versions of some of these numerals appear on pillars built by Ashoka, an Indian king, around 250 BCE. They looked very different from the ones we use today. The symbols for one, two, and three, for instance, were simply horizontal lines.

By the 900s CE, the number one had become a vertical line instead of a horizontal line. Scribes then connected the lines in the numerals for two and three so that they looked much like the modern symbols. This shortcut let scribes avoid lifting their writing tools off the page.

The pillars of Ashoka were built in the 200s BCE, during the reign of King Ashoka. They stood up to 50 feet (15 m) high in locations throughout northern India, Nepal, and Pakistan. Some inscriptions include early versions of modern numerals. Only around twenty of the original pillars still exist.

The numeral for zero (0) probably came into use around 600 CE, joining the other nine numerals.

By about 1100, knowledge of the Indian numbering system had spread. People in other parts of Asia and northern Africa began using these numerals. Different versions of the symbols evolved in each region. Sometimes symbols were rotated from earlier versions.

In eastern Africa and the Middle East, they eventually became the numerals in modern Arabic. In other parts of Asia, the symbols took on their modern forms in the Tibetan, Thai, and Vietnamese scripts. The Indian symbols slowly changed in northern Africa and Spain too. By about 1500, they became the modern numerals that we recognize as 0 through 9.

People in the Middle East learned about these numbers by trading with India. They adapted the system for their own use. By 976 CE, Europeans had learned the system from Arabic merchants in the region that is now Spain. Europeans didn't know about the numerals' roots in ancient India. So they named them Arabic numerals. But now we know that this system originated in India. Since the 1920s, the numeral system has also been known as the Hindu-Arabic system.

The Power of Zero

People in India began using a decimal system around the 500s CE. A decimal system is based on multiples of ten. Most countries use a decimal system. Within a century or two, zero also appeared in the Indian system of mathematics.

This was an important advance in computing. The zero is necessary to the place-value system, which enables numbers to hold different values depending on their placement. Think about the number 220. Each 2 has a different value, depending on its position in the full number. The first 2 stands for 200. The second 2 stands for 20. If a zero weren't on the right, the number would look like 22. The place-value system with zero made adding, subtracting, multiplying, and dividing easy. Numbers could be written one under another in columns and lined up according to value.

Father of Sine

The term *trigonometry* comes from Greek words that mean "the measurement of triangles." Six functions, or ratios, are at the heart of this branch of mathematics. They are used to determine the size and angles of triangles. One of these six functions is called sine.

An ancient Hindu mathematician, Aryabhata the Elder, computed the first known sine tables. These lists showed the value of sine for angles of many sizes. The tables let mathematicians do trigonometry quickly, without stopping to figure out the sine for each angle. Aryabhata included the tables in his book *Aryabhatiya*, written in 499 CE.

In addition to trigonometry, the book included formulas and rules for algebra, geometry, and arithmetic. It included one of the most accurate values of pi that had been found to that time, 3.1416. Aryabhata also introduced a way to find the length of a side of a cube with a known volume. We call this a cube root.

Math and Religion

The Hindu religion, first practiced in what is now northern India, played a big role in encouraging mathematical study. A main theme of the Vedas, sacred Hindu texts, was connecting the heavens, the earth, and the living. Altars were a crucial part of making these connections. The altars came in three shapes that stood for Earth, atmosphere, or space. Together the altars represented the universe. Altars for ritual had to be built in precise shapes and sizes. The numbers of stones or bricks used to build them were related to the length of the lunar and solar years. One altar might have to be circular and measure a certain area. The next altar might have to be a square equal in area to the circular altar. The Vedas provided formulas for constructing altars with precision.

The Vedas are a set of four ancient Hindu religious texts written between 1500 and 500 BCE. Parts of the Vedas describe shapes and sizes of altars based on mathematical principles.

CHAPTER FIVE

Ancient China

The ancient Chinese developed their own decimal system with symbols for the numbers one through nine, like the Hindu-Arabic numeral system. They also likely invented one of the first computing devices, the abacus, to perform complex computing. Some historians argue that Chinese mathematicians discovered some concepts of geometry long before the Greeks made those ideas famous.

Counting Boards and Sticks

The Chinese wrote different kinds of numerals over time. As early as 1500 BCE, ancient priests carved numerals into shells and bones. The inscriptions recorded the number of animals sacrificed, prisoners taken in war, animals hunted, and more. Lines and curves formed the symbols for the numbers one through nine. These combined with symbols for ten, one hundred, and one thousand to make larger numbers.

Beginning around 400 BCE, stick numerals were used in a place-value system. The numbers one to five were

represented with one to five lines. T-shaped figures were used to show the numbers six to nine. The numeral on the right stood for the ones, the next numeral to the left stood for the tens, the next for hundreds, and so on.

Stick numerals likely got their start with counting rods. Math students and scholars in ancient China did calculations with rods on counting boards. The boards were made from wood and were separated into columns or squares. People used sets of red and black counting rods for positive and negative numbers. Each counting rod was about 4 inches (10 cm) long. A full set contained 271 sticks.

Rods were placed on the counting board's squares, with each column from right to left representing the ones, tens, hundreds, thousands, and so forth. Rods that were not carefully placed on the board could cause confusion. So by the 200s CE, stick numbers used lines in alternating directions. The ones numeral, on the right, used vertical lines. The tens column used horizontal lines, then vertical lines for the hundreds, and the pattern repeated. An empty square stood for zero. Sometime after 700 CE, when people in India began using a symbol for zero, use of the symbol entered into China also.

Nine Chapters

The *Jiuzhang Suanshu*, or Nine Chapters on Mathematical Procedures, is the most famous ancient Chinese mathematical text. It dates from between 200 BCE and 50 CE. This ancient work contains 246 math problems. It was a required textbook for math students from the seventh through the twelfth centuries.

Students were required to find proportions and percentages for trading goods. Other sets of problems involved questions of engineering, taxes, and finding costs. Many of the problems in the *Jiuzhang Suanshu* required complicated calculations with fractions.

Astronomy in Ancient Texts

The ancient Chinese took an interest in the movement of heavenly objects. They carefully kept track of changes in the night sky. Chinese records of lunar and solar eclipses are some of the oldest eclipse records in existence.

Astronomy is the focus of one famous Chinese text. The ideas in the *Zhoubi Suanjing* text were collected and put together sometime between 100 BCE and 100 CE, though they were likely much older. Much of the work focuses on measuring the positions and movements of objects in the sky with a gnomon.

Another part of the text discusses side lengths and areas of right triangles. This text explains how the lengths of the sides of a right triangle are related. In geometry this formula

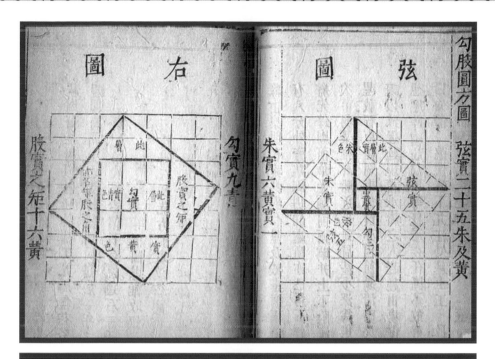

Pages from *Zhoubi Suanjing*, written between 100 BCE and 100 CE, illustrate the Pythagorean Theorem of triangles. This copy of the book was reprinted from the Chinese original in 1603.

is known as the Pythagorean theorem, named for the ancient Greek philosopher Pythagoras. Scholars claimed for many years that Pythagoras had discovered the theorem in ancient Greece. But the material of this book is thought to be older than Pythagoras.

Ancient Computers

The Chinese developed an early version of one of the world's most long-lasting computing devices—the abacus. Early forms of the abacus appeared during the Zhou dynasty, from about 1122 to 256 BCE. But a later version proved more useful. It was in widespread use in China by about 1200 CE. In fact, it is still a popular calculating tool in some parts of Asia.

The abacus could be considered the world's first computer. It was used for addition, subtraction, multiplication, and division. With the abacus, people could perform these calculations much faster.

The abacus consisted of a rectangular frame divided into two parts. Beads slid up and down along a series of vertical rods in each part. Computing with an abacus was simple. With the device flat on a table, the user moved and counted the beads. The person "counted" a bead by moving it toward the

A Chinese abacus uses five beads per rod on the lower deck and two per rod on the upper deck. Abacuses in other countries used different combinations, such as four and one, or ten beads per rod with no divider.

crossbar separating the decks. The upper deck had two beads on each rod. Each of those beads had a value of five. The lower deck had five beads on each rod. Those beads each had a value of one. When five beads on a rod had been counted, the user "carried" the number to the upper deck. This involved moving one of the upper beads to the crossbar and all five lower beads away from it. What happened when both upper beads on a rod had been counted? Simple, the user carried the number to the next rod to the left by moving one of the lower beads toward the crossbar. Each vertical rod represented a place value—ones, tens, hundreds, thousands, and so on.

Calculating Pi

Ancient Chinese mathematicians calculated impressively accurate values of pi. In 264 CE, Liu Hui used a multisided polygon to mimic the shape of a large circle. His polygon had 3,072 sides. He knew how to find the perimeter and radius of that shape, so he could then solve for pi. He found that pi = 3.14159. The true value of pi has endless decimals, but when rounded to five decimal places, this value is exactly right. His calculation was similar, but far more accurate, than the one Archimedes had made nearly four centuries earlier in ancient Greece.

A father-son team of mathematicians figured out an even more precise value in about 480 CE. Zu Chongzhi and Zu Gengzhi found the value of pi to be about 355/113. That's 3.1415929203 when rounded to ten decimal places. It remained the most accurate value of pi for about 1,200 years.

CHAPTER SIX

The Ancient Americas

F or thousands of years, civilizations and empires in the ancient Americas rose and fell, creating their own computation systems along the way. Ancient American groups such as the Maya, Aztec, and Inca developed their own unique counting, math, and astronomical systems completely isolated from Eurasian traditions, using them to build enormous cities and predict astronomical events.

Counting by 20s

The Maya, whose descendants live mainly in modern-day Guatemala, began settling into farming villages before 1200 BCE. Eventually, Maya towns and cities stretched throughout an area in Central America called the Yucatán. The culture thrived from about 200 to 900 CE.

Most modern societies use a decimal system based on the number 10. Place values increase in powers of 10: 1, 10, 100, 1,000, 10,000, 100,000, 1,000,000, and so on. The Maya, however, used a vigesimal system. This is a system based on

The ancient Maya began building the city of Tikal in Guatemala around 800 BCE. It remained a center of religion and politics for the Maya into the 900s CE.

the number 20. In the Mayan system, place values increased in powers of 20: 1, 20, 400, 8,000, 160,000. To build the number 62, the Maya used three twenties and two ones, instead of six tens and two ones as done would in a base-10 numbering system. Anthropologists don't know why the Maya used the base-20 numbering system—perhaps because most people have twenty fingers and toes. Maya numerals consisted of dots and bars. One dot stood for one, and one bar stood for five. The Mayan symbol for zero was a small oval with several lines inside.

Numbers All in a Row

The Maya used a place-value system. Hindu-Arabic numbers increase in value from right to left, with ones in the right-hand

45

A close-up of a panel from the Madrid Codex, a Maya text, clearly shows Mayan numbers from the fourteenth or fifteenth century CE, when the codex was probably written.

position, tens in the next spot, then hundreds, and so on. But in the Maya system, numerals were written from bottom to top. And because the Maya used a base-20 numbering system, values increased in powers of twenty: ones on the bottom row, twenties above them, four hundreds next, and so on.

The Maya Calendar

In Maya culture, some days were lucky—and some unlucky. Lucky days were chosen for important activities such as

Maya Mathematicians

Mathematicians held an honored spot in Maya society. They helped keep the calendar, and they predicted the movements of celestial bodies. They also made business calculations, computing prices of goods and land, for instance. Mathematicians were shown in Mayan glyphs, a picture writing similar to Egyptian hieroglyphics, by a special symbol that included a scroll with numbers. The first mathematician identified in Maya picture-writing was a woman. We don't know her name or anything about her. But she must have been a very important person.

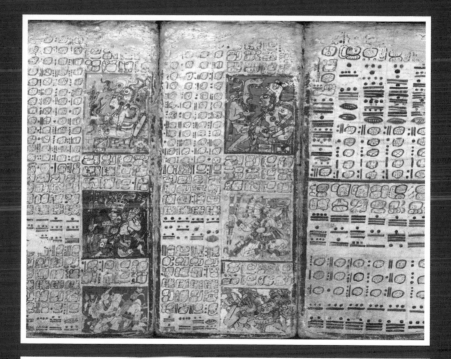

This page from the Dresden Codex shows many Maya numerals. The Dresden Codex, written around the 1100s CE, is a compilation of earlier Maya almanacs and astrological and religious information.

weddings, battles, and planting and harvesting crops. The Maya also celebrated many religious holidays, which had to be observed on the same days each year. To keep track of lucky days and holidays, the Maya needed an accurate calendar—one in step with the solar year.

The Maya used two calendars. The tzolkin, or sacred calendar, contained 260 days. The days were named after Maya gods, thought to carry time across the sky. The tzolkin was used in combination with the haab, a 365-day calendar based on the solar year.

The Maya calendars were complicated. They were based on movements of the sun, the moon, and the planet Venus. Historians do not know exactly how the Maya calendars were developed, but they came into use in the first century CE. Their solar calendar was more accurate than any other calendar in the ancient world.

The Maya also kept track of passing days with a third system, the Long Count. The Maya had calculated what they considered to be the date the world was created. This was August 11, 3113 BCE, by our modern calendar. The Long Count recorded the number of days since that date. Maya numbers show the Long Count date on Stela 29, a stone monument from 292 CE found in the ancient city of Tikal, Guatemala. The Long Count date appears as 8.12.14.8.15— meaning 1,243,615 days since the Maya date of creation.

The Aztec Calendar

Several hundred years after the Maya civilization, the Aztecs became a powerful force in Central America. Between the early 1300s and 1500s CE, they ruled an empire stretching

When the Sun Stone was first discovered in Mexico City, Mexico, in 1790 CE, people thought it was an Aztec calendar. Hieroglyphs carved on the stone refer to special days in the Aztec year. The stone was probably used as an altar.

from modern-day central Mexico to Guatemala, El Salvador, and Honduras. The city of Tenochtitlán, at the site of modern Mexico City, was the heart of the empire.

The Aztec calendar was similar to the Maya calendar. Like the Maya, the Aztecs measured time in three different ways. A 260-day sacred calendar kept track of which Aztec gods ruled over the days and weeks. This was the Tonalpohualli. A 365-day calendar, the Xiuhpohualli, measured the solar year. It kept track of seasons. The start of these two calendars matched up just once every fifty-two years. This stretch of 18,980 days, or fifty-two years, made up the third Aztec calendar.

Inca Counting Ropes

The Inca of South America were a thriving society from about 1400 to 1600 CE. The Inca culture arose separately from the Maya and Aztec civilizations and developed its own computing technology. The Inca are known for their impressive building feats. They built Machu Picchu, an ancient city on a steep mountain ridge in modern-day Peru. Like the Egyptians, the Inca must have used computing technology to keep building projects in order and keep records of workers, supplies, and land. However, most experts believe that the Inca had no writing system. Information was probably passed through word of mouth. They saved this information using the quipu, a group of knotted cords that served as a complex recording device for numbers. Quipus kept track of people counted in a census, a farmer's animals, tax records, and more.

"The Mayan concern for understanding the cycles of the celestial bodies, particularly the sun, the moon and Venus, led them to accumulate a large set of highly accurate observations."

—Luis F. Rodriguez, astronomer, 1985

A quipu had a main horizontal cord with several vertical cords attached to it. Other cords may have been attached to some of those cords, like small branches attached to larger branches on a tree. The Inca recorded information on quipus by tying knots on each cord. Knots of three types and in different points along a cord stood for numbers in different place values, such as hundreds, tens, or ones. Cords of different colors were used to identify the things being counted. The end cord may have shown the total when the other cords' numbers were added together.

CHAPTER SEVEN
Ancient Greece

Ancient Greece was a powerful civilization that conquered much of the Mediterranean and Middle Eastern worlds, from Egypt to the border of India. The Greeks founded the city of Alexandria in Egypt, which became a center for computing and science. The Greeks borrowed some computing technology from the Egyptians, but they also developed entirely new fields of computing. Much of modern mathematics builds on the writings of ancient Greek mathematicians. They laid the foundation for modern mathematics.

The ancient Greeks separated math into two main branches. They used applied math to solve practical problems. Theoretical math involved the study of lines, figures, and points that do not exist in nature. The Greeks also used math to prove and disprove ideas about the natural world.

Greek Numerals

Imagine having to memorize twenty-seven symbols for numbers instead of the ten we use. That's what students in ancient Greece

The Parthenon and other ancient Greek structures from the 400s BCE still stand on the Acropolis, the hill overlooking the modern-day city of Athens, Greece.

did. The Greeks used the twenty-four letters in their alphabet to stand for numbers. When they ran out of their own letters, they borrowed three letters from the Phoenician alphabet. This alphabet was an older alphabet from the area that is now Lebanon, Syria, Palestine, and Israel.

The first nine Greek letters stood for the single-digit numbers, one through nine. The second nine letters represented multiples of ten—ten, twenty, thirty, and so on up to ninety. The last nine letters stood for hundreds, up to nine hundred. A bar placed to the left of a numeral indicated thousands. The letter M below a numeral stood for tens of thousands.

A Famous Theorem

The Greek philosopher Pythagoras lived from about 580 to 500

500 BCE. Pythagoras started a school of math and philosophy in Crotone, in modern-day Italy, which was then part of Greece.

"Geometry is the knowledge of the eternally existent."

—Plato, *Republic*, ca. 380 BCE

For many years, people believed Pythagoras created a theorem about right triangles called the Pythagorean theorem. Historians have found evidence that other cultures had discovered this theorem before Pythagoras was alive. The Babylonians used the equation in surveying land and figuring the area of fields. The *Zhoubi Suanjing* suggests that the Chinese were already aware of it too. But many people still call it the Pythagorean theorem.

Right triangles are triangles that include a 90-degree angle. The side opposite the right angle is called the hypotenuse. The theorem states that the length of the hypotenuse, squared (multiplied by itself), is equal to the sum of the squares of the other two legs of the triangle. We often state the Pythagorean theorem as $a^2 + b^2 = c^2$. In this equation, a and b stand for the legs that form the right angle of the triangle, and c stands for the opposite side, the hypotenuse.

One Theorem Leads to Another

Euclid, another Greek mathematician, taught math in Alexandria. He studied prime numbers. A prime number is one that can be divided evenly only by 1 and itself, such as 3, 7, or 11. Euclid proved that there are an infinite number of prime numbers.

Around 300 BCE, Euclid put together many theorems about geometry, including many from other important mathematicians. He used one theorem to prove another and that theorem to prove the next. But Euclid ran into a problem. If each theorem was proved with an existing theorem, how could a person prove the first theorem? Euclid solved that problem using axioms—statements so obvious that proving them is unnecessary. Two of the axioms that Euclid used were that a straight-line segment can be drawn to connect any two points. Another was that any straight-line segment can be extended to form an endless straight line. Using these axioms, he was able to use angles to determine whether two lines would ever cross or would run parallel to each other forever.

With axioms and theorems, Euclid organized a system of geometry known by modern mathematicians as Euclidean geometry. Euclid put his system into a thirteen-volume book, the *Elements*. It was used as a basic geometry textbook for two thousand years. High school geometry courses are still based on the first volumes of the *Elements*.

Eureka!

Archimedes lived from about 287 to 212 BCE in the city of Syracuse on the island of Sicily. The Roman writer Vitruvius wrote about one discovery of Archimedes. It is a story that may or may not be true, but it shows how his law of buoyancy could be used to measure the volume of irregularly shaped objects. The story goes that the city's ruler, Hiero II, asked Archimedes to find out whether a crown was made of pure gold or a mixture of gold and silver. Archimedes supposedly got the answer while relaxing in the bathtub. He leaped from a tub and ran naked through the streets shouting, "Eureka!" In ancient Greek, that

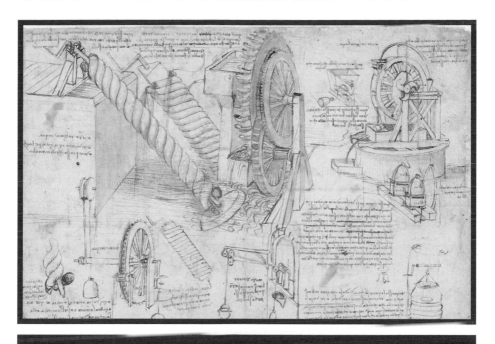

Italian artist and inventor Leonardo da Vinci (1452–1519) was inspired by Archimedes's work with spirals. These are da Vinci's notes and drawings of a screw that Archimedes described in the third century BCE.

means "I have found it."

According to the story, Archimedes realized that a gold or silver object submerged in water would displace, or push aside, water equal to its own volume. Archimedes knew that gold is denser than silver, so a crown of gold and silver would displace more water than a pure gold crown that weighed the same. The gold–and–silver crown would have a greater volume from the extra silver needed to make it weigh the same.

Archimedes dropped pieces of pure gold into water to measure the displacement. Then he dropped in the crown. Sure enough, it displaced more water than the pure gold mass had. Archimedes had figured out that the crown was not made of pure gold.

A Great Math Wizard

Some historians think that Archimedes was one of the ancient world's greatest math wizards. He used math to design machines and made great advances in computing. For example, around 240 BCE, Archimedes computed a new value for pi that was much more accurate than earlier figures. Using an arithmetic formula, he found the perimeter of a ninety-six-sided shape just barely outside a circle. Then he used the formula to find the perimeter of another shape just inside the circle. Archimedes knew the perimeter of the circle would be between those numbers. He probably was the first person to calculate pi this way instead of with actual measurements. This approach, known as the method of exhaustion, gave him better results. He found that pi is between 3 1/7 (about 3.1429) and 3 10/71 (about 3.1408). Mathematicians used this figure for centuries.

Archimedes studied spirals and developed special math techniques. Centuries later, these techniques became the

Father of Algebra

Diophantus was a Greek mathematician who lived in Alexandria around 275 CE. Diophantus has been called the father of algebra. He introduced the use of symbols and equations (such as $x + y = z$) in math and wrote *Arithmetica*, the world's first collection of writings on algebra, in the third century CE.

basis for a new field of math called integral calculus. Integral calculus is used to find area, volume, and other measurements by combining very small data points.

Hypatia of Alexandria

The first female mathematician known by name was Hypatia. She was born around 370 CE in Alexandria, a Greek colony in Egypt. She became one of the most famous mathematicians in the ancient world. Hypatia led a large group of philosophers and scientists in Alexandria. She became a political advisor for the city of Alexandria, taught philosophy and astronomy, and wrote many commentaries on many famous works of mathematics as

This terra-cotta sculpture of Greek mathematician Hypatia was made in the 400s CE.

well as her own book on astronomy. Hypatia also built astrolabes to help ships navigate and hydrometers to measure the density of liquids.

An angry mob murdered Hypatia in 415 CE, and many mathematicians and scientists fled Alexandria after Hypatia's murder. They probably feared that they, too, would be killed. Before Hypatia's murder, Alexandria had been the world's center of science, medicine, and learning for almost seven hundred years. Hypatia's tragic death marked the end of Alexandria as the global center of learning.

Tick Tock, Better Clocks

A Greek engineer named Ctesibius of Alexandria made an early form of our modern mechanical clock in the second century BCE. It was a clepsydra, or water clock, which was more accurate than a sundial and could tell time at night or indoors. Ctesibius's clock consisted of a float with statue a on top. The float was placed in a container of water. It rose as water steadily dripped into the container. The statue held a pointer in its hand and showed the time by pointing to lines on the inside of the container. When the water reached the top of the container, it flowed out to start again, and the float with the statue on top moved down to its original position.

The Tower of the Winds

Big Ben is a 13-ton (11.8 t) bell in the clock tower of the Houses of Parliament in London, England. People have used it to keep track of the time since 1859. The Tower of the Winds in ancient Athens held giant sundials. It was the ancient world's Big Ben.

Also known as the Horologion of Andronikos Kyrrhestes, the Tower of the Winds is still standing. It is a marble tower 42 feet (13 m) high and 26 feet (8 m) across.

Andronicus of Cyrrhus, a Greek astronomer and mathematician, designed the tower around 100 BCE. It has eight sides, each of which had a sundial high on the wall so people nearby could easily see the movement of shadows and tell the time. Using geometry, Andronicus computed exactly how shadows would fall onto the surfaces of each wall to design the sundial lines. For telling time at night and on cloudy days, Andronicus added a clepsydra inside the tower.

An Ancient Computer?

In 1901 divers swimming off the Greek island of Antikythera found the remains of an unusual mechanical device. It came from the wreck of a ship that had sunk two thousand years earlier. The device became known as the Antikythera mechanism.

Nobody knew what the device was until the 1970s. Then, a Yale University scientist, Derek J. de Solla Price, concluded that it was an ancient computer. It had thirty gears, as well as pointers and dials. The machinery turned to calculate the rising and setting of the sun and the moon and movements of important stars. De Solla Price thought that the Antikythera mechanism was probably displayed in a museum or public hall, where it amazed visitors.

In 2005 scientists from Greece and the United Kingdom studied the inside of the Antikythera mechanism with new cutting-edge technology. The new technology captured images of ancient inscriptions so faint that no one had seen

This is one of the gears from the Antikythera mechanism, which was recovered from the bottom of the sea in 1901. The device, made in the second century BCE, is a series of bronze gears that may have been used in navigation.

them since the device sank with the ship. These inscriptions shed light on the functions of the mechanism. The ancient computer predicted solar eclipses and even kept track of the four-year cycle of the ancient Olympic Games. In addition, dials on the back of the mechanism bear the names of the twelve months of an ancient calendar. The names have origins in Sicily. Scientists think these names may connect the Antikythera mechanism to Sicily's most famous mathematician, Archimedes.

Who was the brilliant designer of this ancient computer? It remains a mystery. One thing is certain—it was the most advanced computing device for more than a thousand years.

CHAPTER EIGHT

Ancient Rome

Ancient Rome began as a small town, founded in 753 BCE, located on the Tiber River in central Italy. Gradually, the Romans conquered neighboring lands and built a great empire that eventually stretched from the Caspian Sea and Red Sea in the east, across northern Africa to Spain in the west, and to England in the north. Like many other ancient civilizations, the Romans learned about technology from other cultures, including the people they conquered.

In fact, the Romans inherited much of their computing technology from the Greeks. Using the groma and other surveying instruments borrowed from the conquered Egyptians, the Romans constructed roads, buildings, and other structures.

Roman Numerals

The Romans developed a numbering system known as Roman numerals. It used just seven letters from the Latin alphabet, and a

This painting shows an artist's recreation of the forum in ancient Rome. The ancient Romans were masters of engineering and architecture. Many of their structures are still standing.

few extra symbols could be used to write any number. The Latin letter *I* stood for one, *V* for five, *X* for ten, *L* for fifty, *C* for one hundred, *D* for five hundred, and *M* for one thousand.

Placing a small bar over the top of a number multiplied its value by one thousand. For instance, M (1,000) with a bar on top meant one million. In theory, a person could add enough bars to write huge numbers. In practice, the Romans rarely used more than one bar.

Roman numerals were written from left to right. A number placed to the right of another number of equal or greater value indicated addition. That is, VI meant 5 + 1, or 6. MD meant 1,000 + 500, or 1,500. A number placed to the left of another number of greater value indicated subtraction.

For example, XL meant 50 – 10, or 40. MCM meant 1,000 + (1,000 – 100), or 1,900.

Roman numerals do have a few disadvantages compared to other number systems. They take up a lot of space, for instance. They also are hard to use for addition, subtraction, multiplication, and division. Roman numerals are still used for each Super Bowl and Olympic Games. Some clock faces and chapter markings in books also use them.

How Far Have We Come?

Many dashboards on modern cars have digital displays, but one of their most important displays comes from the ancient world. The odometer keeps track of a car's mileage, or how far it has travelled. Vitruvius, a Roman engineer who lived from 70 to 25 BCE, invented the first odometer. He mounted a large wheel in a frame, much like a modern wheelbarrow. The wheel was attached to a gear with four hundred notches. With each turn of the wheel, the gear moved ahead one notch. The gear moved four hundred times every five thousand Roman feet, equal to one Roman mile. And with each four hundred turns, a stone dropped into a metal container. The clang of the stone signaled that one Roman mile had passed.

Updated Calendars

The first Roman calendar, developed around 738 BCE, was based on the lunar year. It had only 304 days, divided into ten months. That made it sixty-one days shorter than the solar year. Later, the Romans added two more months, but the year was still not long enough. To make up for the shortfall, the Romans

This reconstruction of an ancient Roman odometer was created based on the descriptions of the device by the Greek mathematician Hero of Alexandria, Egypt (a Roman city at the time), and Roman Marcus Vitruvius Pollio. These engineers lived around the same time in the first century BCE.

had to add an extra month to their calendar every two years.

The Roman calendar got further off track when government officials added even more extra months. Why? Sometimes they did it to stay in office longer or delay elections. Finally, in 45 BCE, Emperor Julius Caesar adopted the Egyptian solar calendar for the Roman Empire. He called it the Julian calendar in his own honor. It had a year of 365 days, and every fourth year had an extra day. The Julian calendar was only eleven minutes and fourteen seconds longer than the solar year.

CONCLUSION
After the Ancients

It may be surprising how much of our computing technology has roots in the ancient world. Our modern numbering system is based on the number ten. But the Mesopotamian numbering system, based on sixty, remains in our daily lives as well. We still use sixty as a base measurement for time. A minute has sixty seconds. An hour has sixty minutes. Degrees (units of measurement for angles) are also based on the number sixty. A circle contains 360 degrees, which is 60 x 6.

Beam scales are another example of ancient Babylonian computing technology that have lasted. Many scales used in doctors' offices are beam scales. And in some places, shopkeepers and others still use abacuses. Over time and around the globe, these simple computers have held their own against digital technology.

Variations on the abacus are still used in Russia and Japan. The US Army tested the usefulness of the Japanese abacus in 1946. It compared the abacus to a digital calculator in a test of speed and accuracy. Each machine had a skilled operator to solve problems using addition, subtraction, multiplication, and division. The abacus won, 4 points to 1!

Building on Ancient Ideas

With time, of course, people improved upon many types of computing technology. One example is the calendar used in most countries around the world. People throughout the Roman Empire used the Julian Calendar for more than 1,500 years after Julius Caesar introduced it in 45 BCE. But over time, the calendar's eleven-minute-per-year error accumulated into days. Holidays were occurring at the wrong time of year.

A newer calendar, known as the Gregorian calendar, was almost exactly as long as the solar year. This calendar used the designations BC and AD, based on the Christian timeline of the birth of Jesus Christ. A monk had devised this year-numbering system in 525 CE. BC stands for "before Christ." AD stands for the Latin words *anno Domini*, or "in the year of our Lord." Most of the world uses this calendar. However, AD and BC have been replaced to make writing more inclusive to people of all cultures and faiths. Historians now use CE ("of the Common Era") and BCE ("before the Common Era").

By the 1600s, ancient technology had become the basis for other new developments in math. In 1619 the French mathematician René Descartes invented coordinate geometry. He studied geometry on a coordinate (numbered) grid, using principles of algebra. This led to more advanced geometry. It enabled mathematicians to use equations to create and change lines, planes, or shapes within the grid.

French mathematicians Pierre de Fermat and Blaise

Pascal developed the mathematical concept of probability in 1654. Probability involves counting the number of possible outcomes in a situation to determine how likely a certain outcome is. When you flip a coin, it can land on one of two sides. So the probability of it landing heads-up is one in two. Probability is an important concept in weather forecasting, online games, and other areas.

Calculus, a field of math that involves how things change, developed around a decade later. Calculus is used to define curves, areas, volumes, and movement. In 1665 Isaac Newton, a British scientist and mathematician, showed how the two central operations in calculus relate to each other. The German philosopher and mathematician Gottfried Leibniz also developed this field independently of Newton. In the 1670s, he developed an approach that many calculus students still learn to write equations. Calculus paved the way for countless advances in engineering and mechanics, physics, statistics, astronomy, economics, medicine, and more.

From Mathematics to Computers

Mathematicians have continued to build and improve on one another's ideas over time. But how did we get from calculus to laptops and smartphones?

The abacus and the Antikythera mechanism were early versions of calculators or computers. Digital computers are programmable versions of these machines. We can program them to perform all kinds of operations. Early programmable machines appeared in the early 1800s. One of the most famous was the Jacquard textile loom, which used punch cards to control how threads were woven into

This photo of the Electronic Numerical Integrator and Computer (ENIAC), an early electronic computer from the 1940s, shows the size of early digital computers. Part of the ENIAC is held by the Smithsonian Institute.

cloth in specific patterns. The first mechanical computer, the Analytical Engine, was invented by the English mathematician and engineer Charles Babbage around the same time. Ada Lovelace, another English mathematician, wrote a program ordering the machine to calculate a sequence of numbers called Bernoulli numbers. It is considered the first algorithm, or set of instructions, ever invented to run a computer.

Alan Turing was a British mathematician, cryptographer, and computer scientist who worked during the 1930s and 40s. He helped to crack secret codes during World War II and made huge advances in the practical use of computers. Turing also invented a hypothetical machine called the

Turing Machine, which could run any algorithm using only a long tape marked with ones and zeroes. This is called the binary numeral system. Binary code uses patterns of zeroes and ones to represent numbers, text, and other information. For example, the number nine in the decimal system becomes 1001 in binary code. All modern computers use binary code. This work earned him the nickname "the father of computer science."

However, an American named George Stibitz shares that honor with Turing. In 1937 he built the first calculator that used the binary numeral system, or binary code, to perform arithmetic.

As electronic, digital computers advanced throughout the 1900s, they grew both in capability and size. Scientists developed hardware to store information. This changed computers from calculators into data storage machines, as we know them. Room-size computers were built throughout the 1950s and 1960s to process advanced calculations. Then, in the 1970s, the invention of microprocessors allowed computers to shrink dramatically. By the 1980s, personal computers could fit on a desktop. In the early 2000s, the first smartphones became widely available and allowed people to hold a computer in the palm of their hand.

Thanks to the incredible speed of computers, we can work thousands of times faster and more efficiently than ever before. The average smartphone, for instance, has more computing power than a room-sized computer from the mid-20th century. This is possible because of the computing technology that started in the ancient world. Those early systems for measuring, counting, and calculating built the foundation for the laptops, smartphones, and other computing wonders we use every day.

TIMELINE

ca. 35000 BCE   Early African peoples in the modern-day country of Swaziland carve notches into a baboon bone as a way to track numbers. This is later known as the Lebombo bone.

ca. 3500 BCE   Egyptians begin using obelisks as early sundials.

ca. 3000 BCE   Mesopotamians write on clay tablets, including number symbols from their counting system based on 60. These are some of the world's earliest known number symbols. Egyptians begin using Nilometers to measure the water level during the Nile River's annual flood.

ca. 2000 BCE   Babylonian and Egyptian mathematicians discover the concept of pi. They calculate the first approximate values.

ca. 1900–1600 BCE   Babylonians write calculations on tablets that make use of the Pythagorean theorem thousands of years before Pythagoras was born.

ca. 1500 BCE   Egyptians design the first clepsydra, or water clock.

ca. 1400 BCE   Sumerians use surveying to measure land boundaries.

500s BCE   According to some ancient texts, Pythagoras proves that for any right triangle, the square of the length of the hypotenuse is equal to the sum of the squares of the other two sides. This becomes known as the Pythagorean theorem.

ca. 300 BCE   Babylonian astronomer Berosus creates a sundial by placing a gnomon in a bowl-shaped base. Lines on the base divide the day into twelve equal parts.

Greek mathematician Euclid publishes the geometry text *Elements*. This includes five axioms on which he bases some of his theorems.

240 BCE   With his method of exhaustion, Archimedes uses a 96-sided polygon to determine that the value of pi (π) is between 3 1/7 (about 3.1429) and 3 10/71 (about 3.1408).

238 BCE	The pharaoh Ptolemy III improves the Egyptian 365-day calendar by adding one extra day every four years. The new calendar is about eleven minutes longer than the solar year.
200 BCE–50 CE	The Chinese classic text *Jiuzhang Suanshu* is made from collected ancient writings, including an explanation of the Pythagorean theorem perhaps developed separately from the Greek tradition.
100s BCE	Greek engineer Ctesibius creates a new kind of clepsydra that is more precise and accurate than older versions.
300s CE	The Maya of Central America use zero as part of their base-20 numbering system.
499	Aryabhata the Elder, of India, includes tables of sine values for many angles in his book, *Aryabhatiya*.
500s	People in India begin using Hindu-Arabic numerals in a decimal system.
ca. 1200	The abacus becomes popular in China, although earlier versions had existed for centuries.
ca. 1400–1600	The Inca use knotted ropes called quipus to keep records of numbers and other information.
1858	Alexander Henry Rhind finds a mathematical papyrus near Thebes, Egypt. The Rhind Mathematical Papyrus dates to about 1650 BCE.
1901	Divers find the Antikythera mechanism in a shipwreck.
1946	The US Army pits the Japanese abacus against an electric calculator in a contest of speed and accuracy. The Japanese abacus wins.
1970s	Archaeologists find the ancient Lebombo bone near Border Cave in Swaziland.
2005	Greek and British scientists study the Antikythera mechanism with new imaging technology. They reveal inscriptions that give clues about the many uses and the origin of the mechanism.

GLOSSARY

algebra: a branch of mathematics that deals with quantities expressed in symbols

archaeologist: a person who studies material remains (such as tools, pottery, jewelry, stone walls, and monuments) of past human life and activities

axiom: a statement accepted as true that serves as a basis for further arguments or theorems

base-10: involving a numbering system in which place values increase in powers of 10

dynasty: a powerful group or family that maintains its position for a considerable time

geometry: a branch of mathematics that deals with the measurement, properties, and relationships of points, lines, angles, surfaces, and solids

lunar year: a time period based on the phases of the moon, lasting a total of 354 days. The lunar year was divided into twelve months of 29 or 30 days each.

mathematics: the science of numbers and their operation

numeral: a symbol used to represent a number

pi: the ration of the circumference of a circle to its diameter

place-value system: a numeral system in which numerals hold different values depending on their placement

polygon: a closed plane figure bounded by straight lines

prime number: a number that can be divided evenly only by 1 and itself

right angle: an angle whose sides are perpendicular to each other and measuring 90 degrees

sequence: an ordered list of objects or numbers in which repetitions are allowed

surveying: using mathematics to measure the size and elevation of fields, mountains, valleys, and other physical formations

theorem: a statement in mathematics that has been proved or is to be proved

trigonometry: the study of the properties of triangles

SOURCE NOTES

21   "insight into all that exists, knowledge of all secrets.":
        Ahmes the Scribe, the Rhind Papyrus, quoted in Eli Maor,
        Trigonometric Delights (Princeton, NJ: Princeton University
        Press, 1998), 5, available online at http://press.princeton.edu/
        books/maor/prologue.pdf (July 15, 2010).

26   "For the Egyptians . . . proceeded from utility.": Proclus
        Lycius, *A Commentary on the First Book of Euclid's Elements*,
        trans. Glenn R. Morrow (Princeton, NJ: Princeton University
        Press, 1970).

42   "Of all the . . . can be done.": Georges Ifrah, *The Universal
        History of Computing* (New York: John Wiley and Sons,
        2001), 24.

50   "The Mayan concern . . . highly accurate observations.": L.
        F. Rodríguez, Astronomy among the Mayans (Spanish), Rev.
        Mexicana Astronom. Astrofis. 10 (1985), 443–453, available
        online at MacTutor History of Mathematics, trans. John J.
        O'Connor and Edmund F. Robertson, http://www-history.
        mcs.st-and.ac.uk/HistTopics/Mayan_mathematics.html (July
        14, 2010).

53   "Geometry is the knowledge of the eternally existent.": Stewart
        Shapiro, *The Oxford Handbook of Philosophy of Mathematics
        and Logic* (New York: Oxford University Press, 2005), 243.

SELECTED BIBLIOGRAPHY

Adkins, Lesley, and Roy A. Adkins. *Handbook to Life in Ancient Rome.* New York: Facts on File, 1994.

Asimov, Isaac. *Asimov on Numbers.* Garden City, NY: Doubleday, 1977.

Benson, Elizabeth P. *The Maya World.* New York: Thomas Y. Crowell Company, 1977.

Fauvel, John, and Jeremy Gray, eds. *The History of Mathematics: A Reader.* New York: Macmillan, 1987.

Fleet, Simon. *Clocks.* London: Octopus Books, 1972.

Grimal, Nicolas. *A History of Ancient Egypt.* Cambridge, MA: Blackwell Publishers, 1994.

Heilbron, J. L. *Geometry Civilized: History, Culture, and Technique.* New York: Oxford University Press, 1998.

Hodges, Henry. *Technology in the Ancient World.* New York: Alfred A. Knopf, 1977.

Hollingdale, Stuart. *Makers of Mathematics.* New York: Penguin Books, 1991.

Ingpen, Robert, and Philip Wilkinson. *Encyclopedia of Ideas That Changed the World: The Greatest Discoveries and Inventions of Human History.* New York: Penguin Books, 1993.

James, Peter, and Nick Thorpe. *Ancient Inventions.* New York: Ballantine Books, 1994.

Novikov, Igor D. *The River of Time.* Cambridge: Cambridge University Press, 1998.

O'Connor, John J., and Edmund F. Robertson. "Mayan Mathematics." MacTutor History of Mathematics Archive. http://www-history.mcs.st-and.ac.uk/HistTopics/Mayan_mathematics.html (September 14, 2010).

Robinson, Andrew. *The Story of Writing.* New York: Thames & Hudson, 1995.

Saggs, H. W. F. *Civilization Before Greece and Rome.* New Haven, CT: Yale University Press, 1989.

FURTHER READING

Books

Connor-Smith, Jennifer. *The Wide World of Coding: The People and Careers behind the Programs*. Minneapolis: Twenty-First Century Books, 2020.
Learn about the world of software programs and the people who create them in this thoroughly researched book that explores the computation and careers of coding.

Estes, Fred. *Teen Innovators: Nine Young People Engineering a Better World with Creative Inventions*. Minneapolis: Zest Books, 2022.
Discover how science and math can be used to engineer solutions to problems in your community and beyond through these nine stories of teen inventors.

Ignotofsky, Rachel. *The History of the Computer: People, Inventions, and Technology that Changed Our World*. Berkeley: Ten Speed Press, 2022.
Uncover the development of the computer from the abacus to the first commercial computers of the 1950s to the modern smartphone.

Latchana Kenney, Karen. *Folding Tech: Using Origami and Nature to Revolutionize Technology*. Minneapolis: Twenty-First Century Books, 2021.
Discover how the ancient art of paper folding is inspiring today's technology in this in-depth look at the math and history behind folding technologies.

Levy, Joel. *Exploring the Mysteries of Mathematics*. New York: Rosen Publishing, 2017.
Learn about how mathematic concepts like the quadratic equation were discovered and used throughout history.

Websites

Ancient Worlds

https://www.pbs.org/wgbh/nova/topic/ancient/
This companion website to the PBS television series *NOVA* investigates archaeological and architectural mysteries of the ancient world, from the Great Pyramid of Giza to the Maya metropolis Caracol.

Build an Archimedes Screw

https://www.sciencebuddies.org/stem-activities/build-archimedes-screw
This site gives you step-by-step instructions to make your own Archimedes screw. Learn how to use water to move objects just like the ancient Greek mathematician Archimedes.

The Coriolis Effect: Earth's Rotation and Its Effect on Weather

https://education.nationalgeographic.org/resource/coriolis-effect
This article explores how the Coriolis Effect is measured and studied by people around the world. Learn how pilots find the quickest routes and scientists study weather on Earth and other planets using the Coriolis Effect.

A Master of the Grandfather Clock Reveals Time's Hidden History

https://www.nationalgeographic.com/history/article/a-master-of-the-grandfather-clock-reveals-times-hidden-history
Learn about the history of measuring time, from ancient Roman sundials to modern-day clocks and watches, in this article from *National Geographic*.

INDEX

ABOUT THE AUTHORS

Michael Woods is a science and medical journalist in Washington, DC. He has won many national writing awards. Mary B. Woods is a school librarian. Their past books include the fifteen–volume *Disasters Up Close* series and many titles in the *Seven Wonders* series. The Woodses have four children. When not writing, reading, or enjoying their seven grandchildren, the Woodses travel to gather material for future books.

PHOTO ACKNOWLEDGMENTS

Maskot/Getty Images, p. 5; Jeff Foott/Photodisc/Getty Images, p. 6; Joeykentin/Wikimedia Commons (CC BY-SA 4.0), p. 9; Bettmann/Getty Images, p. 10; Sunday Oladokun/Shutterstock, p. 11; funkyfood London - Paul Williams/Alamy, p. 13; fullempty/Shutterstock, p. 14; Vassil/Wikimedia Commons (CC0 1.0), p. 15; Science History Images/Alamy, p. 17; World History Archive/Alamy, p. 19; Premier/Alamy, p. 21; Print Collector/Hulton Archive/Getty Images, pp. 22, 68; Walter Rawlings/Alamy, p. 24; Science & Society Picture Library/Getty Images, p. 25; GC Stock/Alamy, p. 27; J.D. Dallet/Alamy, p. 28; DEA PICTURE LIBRARY/De Agostini/Getty Images, p. 30; Robert Harding World Imagery/Alamy, p. 33; Dr. Suresh Vasant/Alamy, p. 34; Education Images/Alamy, p. 37; Science History Images/Alamy, p. 39; Pictures from History/Universal Images Group/Getty Images, p. 41; Cheryl Chan/Moment/Getty Images, p. 42; Michael Godek/Moment/Getty Images, p. 45; Peter Horree/Alamy, p. 46; history_docu_photo/Alamy, p. 47; Felix Lipov/Alamy, p. 49; Georgios Alexandris/Alamy, p. 52; Universal Art Archive/Alamy, p. 55; Ancient Art and Architecture/Alamy, pp. 57, 60; FALKENSTEINFOTO/Alamy, p. 62; Gts-tg/Wikimedia Commons (CC BY-SA 4.0), p. 64.

Cover: Science & Society Picture Library/Getty Images.